Alan Turing's
LOGIC GAMES
FOR KIDS

ARCTURUS

This edition published in 2022 by Arcturus Publishing Limited
26/27 Bickels Yard, 151–153 Bermondsey Street,
London SE1 3HA

Author: Gemma Barder
Editor: William Potter
Illustrator: Gareth Conway
Designer: Trudi Webb
Design Manager: Jessica Holliland
Managing Editor: Joe Harris

ISBN: 978-1-3988-2070-8
CH010457NT
Supplier 29, Date 0922, PI 00002623
Printed in China

What is STEM?

STEM is a world-wide initiative that aims to cultivate an interest in Science, Technology, Engineering, and Mathematics, in an effort to promote these disciplines to as wide a variety of students as possible.

Hello, I'm Alan! Welcome to my brain-boggling book! Inside you'll find challenging logic puzzles, picture games to hone your observation skills, mathematical mind-benders to boost your number know-how, and drawing activities to give you a break and recharge. Have fun!

ALL ABOUT ALAN

Alan Turing was born in London in 1912. He was a mathematical genius whose ideas helped develop modern computing.

During World War II, Alan played an important role at Bletchley Park in the UK. He helped design a machine called the "Bombe." The machine was used to decode messages from the German military.

Alan Turing's code-breaking skills helped the Allies shorten the war and saved many lives.

THE TURING TRUST

When you buy this book, you are supporting The Turing Trust. This is a charity, set up by Alan's family, in his memory.

The Turing Trust works with communities in Africa to give people access to computers.

Racehorse reshuffle

Take a look at these racehorses as they dash for the finish line. The winner is the horse that is slightly different from the rest. Spot the difference, and the winner.

Alan Turing's Challenge

How many years ago were the first horse races? Use the code a = 1, b = 2, c = 3, and so on to find out.

20 23 15   20 8 15 21 19 1 14 4,

19 5 22 5 14   8 21 14 4 18 5 4

Space walk

Guide the astronaut through the maze to reach her spaceship.

Tech talk

Read the clues to identify each robot.
Make a cross below its picture, level with its name.

Bolt				
Megadroid				
Robbo				
Axel				

Clues

1 Bolt is not green.

2 Robbo and Bolt have just two arms.

3 Axel is smaller than all the rest.

4 Megadroid has two feet.

Pizza perfection

To complete this picture, shade in the squares to make a perfect reflection on both sides of the green line.

Alan Turing's Challenge

Use a mirror to decode the message below!

Pizza was the first item to be bought over the internet.

Falling leaves

These leaves come in sets of three,
except one leaf which is unique.
Can you spot it?

On the run

Help these runners to plan their routes by adding the missing roads to this map.

1. Draw straight lines from each circle.

2. The number of lines from each circle must exactly match the number inside.

3. No paths should cross.

4. You should be able to travel from one number to any other using the paths.

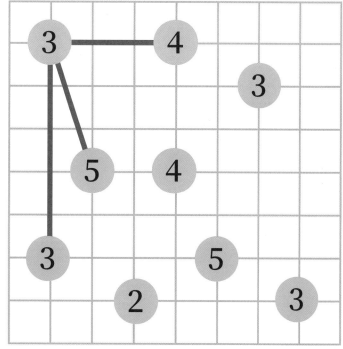

The first three lines have been done for you.

Alan Turing's Challenge

What is the mode of the numbers in the circles? Remember, the mode is the number that appears most often in any set of numbers.

School essentials

Can you fit each of these school supplies just once into each row and column? Sketch them in place.

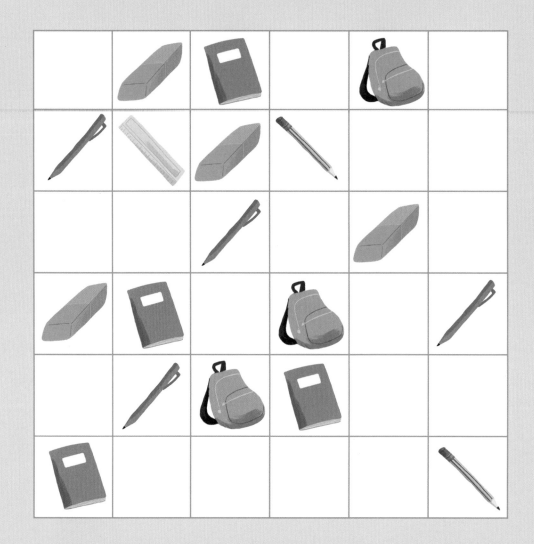

Backpack factor

Can you put this picture back together? Write the number for each piece in the empty grid. You will not need every piece.

Alan Turing's Challenge

Once you have completed the puzzle, make a note of all the leftover numbers. What do they all have in common?

Riveting riddles

Can you answer these tricky questions?

1. What runs up and down but never moves?

2. What gets wetter the more it dries?

3. Jim's father has three sons: Martin, Joe, and what's the name of the third?

4. What question can you never answer truthfully?

5. The more there is, the less you see. What is it?

6. If you were in a race, and you passed the person in second place, which position would you be in?

Letter drop

The postal worker delivers letters in a different order each day.

Can you work out which letter will come next?

Monday

Tuesday

Wednesday

Jargon buster

The teacher has written a message on the board, but it doesn't look quite right! Cross out the extra words to read the message.

The egg giraffe tickets all smell for laugh perfect today's special dinner concert should told have orange teacup sold hamster cage out. Forest monkey Try gerbil race again football monster tomorrow.

Alan Turing's Challenge

Can you make up a sentence using some of the words you've taken from the teacher's board? How many words can you use?

Spotty spot

Every giraffe's pattern is different, just like our fingerprints are different. Look at the close-up. Which giraffe does it belong to?

Take it to the top

What time did these mountaineers reach the summit? They started at 10am.

First stage: 1 hour, 40 minutes

Second stage: 25 minutes

Third stage: 70 minutes

Busiest bee

This busy bee has flown too far from the hive. Move from the Start, following the directions of the arrows, one square at a time, to find where the hive is on the grid.

↑ ↑ ↑ ↑ → → ↑ → ↑ ↑ → ↓ ↓ → → ↑ ↑ ← ← ← ←

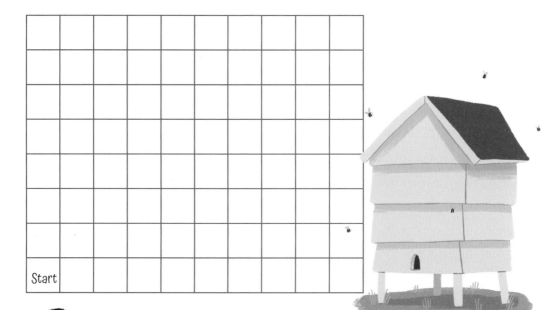

Start

Alan Turing's Challenge

Think up another spot for the bee to go. Plot out a route using symbols as we have done and see if a friend or family member can find it.

Diving differences

Can you spot 8 differences between these two scuba scenes?

Market baskets

Each of these fruits fits perfectly into an L-shaped basket of four joined squares. Draw outlines around each of the four fruits until the grid is complete. The first three baskets have been done for you.

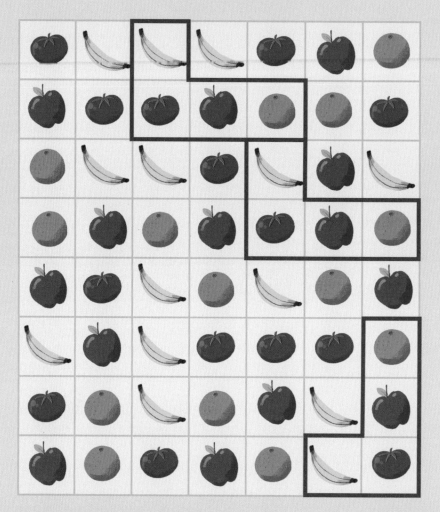

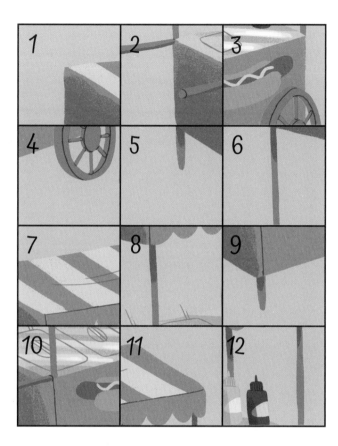

Fast food fix-up

Help cook up some hot dogs. Write the numbers for the mixed-up pieces on the left in the empty grid, below, to show where they belong.

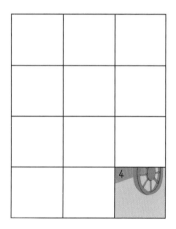

Alan Turing's Challenge

True or false: Hot dogs have been sent into space!

Eggstra-tricky

Look at the groups of eggs below. Can you find them all in the big picture?

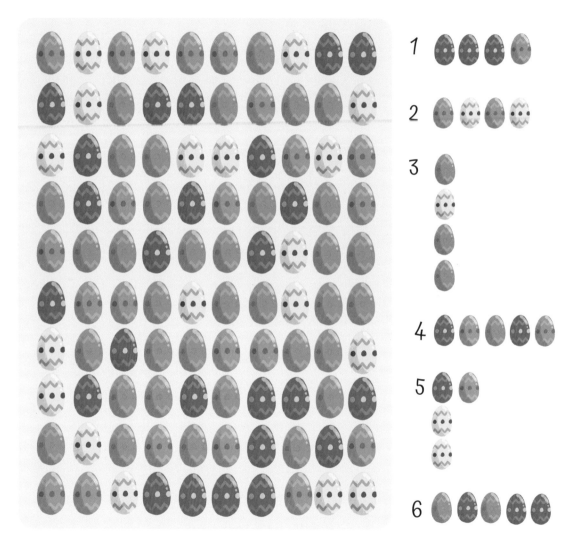

Ali has carved a pumpkin for her best friend. Follow the directions to place the pumpkin at the correct house.

Happy Halloween

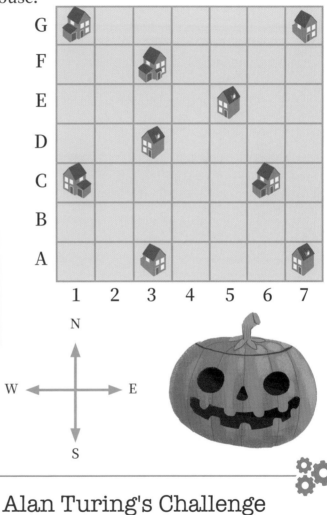

Start at A1

East two spaces

North three spaces

West two spaces

North three spaces

East four spaces

South two spaces

West one space

South two spaces

East three spaces

North four spaces

Alan Turing's Challenge

Pick another house on the grid. Can you write your own coordinates to get there from the starting position?

Funky fish

Complete these puzzles to work out what each of fish should look like.

Fish 1: A two digit number where the first number is greater than the second.

Fish 2: An even number less than 10 but higher than 6.

Fish 3: A prime number.

Fish 4: The number of sides on a hexagon.

Alan Turing's Challenge

Place the four fishy numbers in a line to make the biggest number you can.

Pizza path

To find your way from top to bottom through this pizza-perfect grid, you must follow this sequence of toppings! You can move up, down and across but not diagonally.

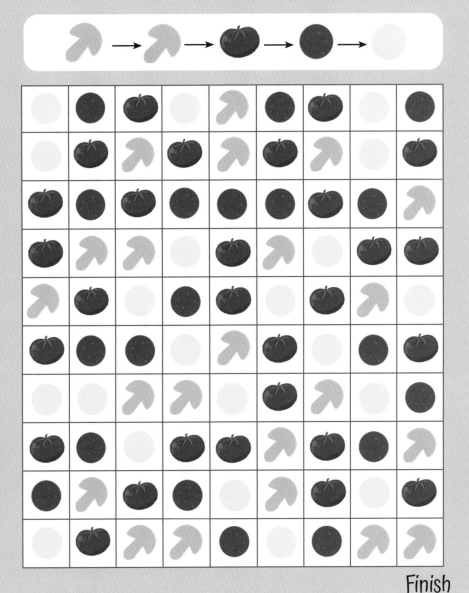

Finish

Mystery machine

Turn each dial following the inventor's instructions to make their latest invention come to life!

Mark on each dial where the arrow should be after …

Dial 1. Half a turn clockwise. A quarter turn back. Then 180° turn clockwise.

Dial 2. All the way round to the 6 o'clock position. A quarter turn clockwise. Then repeat the last move.

Dial 3. Move to the 9 o'clock position. One quarter turn clockwise. Then a 180° turn clockwise.

Dial 4. A half turn clockwise then a 270° turn back. One quarter turn clockwise.

1   2   3   4

Alan Turing's Challenge

Imagine a really amazing machine of your own. What would it do? How would it be powered?

The right notes

None of the instruments in the music shop have price tags on them. Look at the calculations to work out how much each instrument costs.

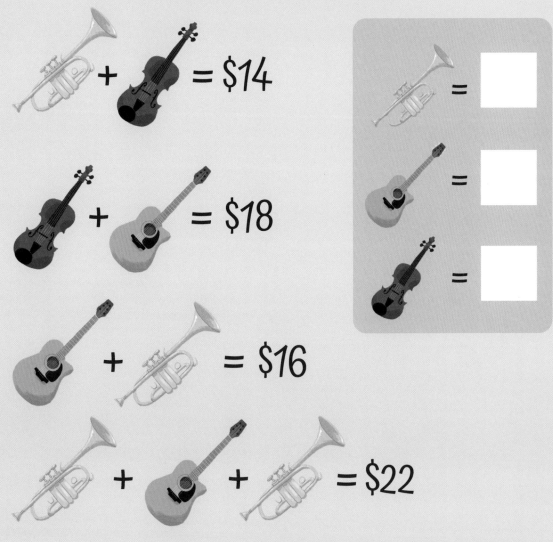

Wizarding wands

Can you turn these four squares into three,
moving only three wands? You won't need magic—
just a little bit of logic!

Alan Turing's Challenge

Can you move two wands so the four
squares become seven squares?

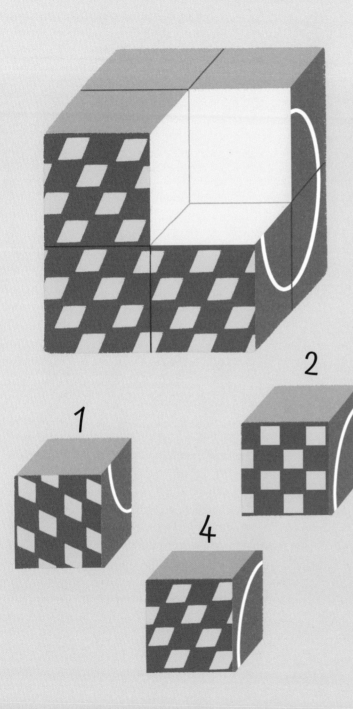

From the block

Take a look at the five small cubes. Which one will fit into the puzzle perfectly?

1

2

3

4

5

Snaking path

Find a safe path through the jungle without stepping on any snakes!

Start

Finish

Join the fours

Write the numbers 1 to 4 in each row, column, and linked circles without a number repeating.

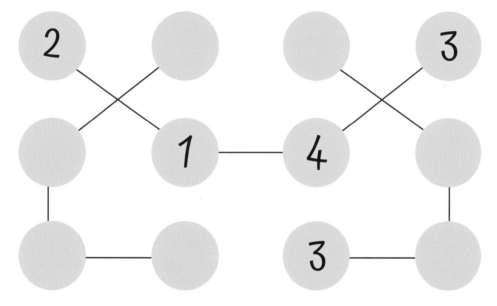

Alan Turing's Challenge

Try making your own puzzle. Copy the grid of circles. Draw lines to connect the circles in groups of 4, then add numbers in pencil. Keep a note of the solution, then erase some of the numbers and give it to a friend to solve!

Precious things

Lady Hamilton-Smythe has her trinkets box in a muddle! How many bracelets, necklaces, and rings can you see?

Riddle me this!

Can you solve more of Alan's testing riddles?

1. This belongs to you, but other people use it more than you do.

2. What has hands, but never claps?

3. You can catch it, but you can't throw it. What is it?

4. What has a head and tail, but no body?

5. What breaks if you don't keep it?

6. Which word becomes shorter by adding two letters?

Precise potions

Each of these potions weighs a different amount. Can you label the blue and orange bottles with their correct number?

Dog daze

These dogs are all having fun in the park. Can you spot the dog that doesn't look like any of the others?

Alan Turing's Challenge

Using the code 1 = a, 2 = b, c = 3, etc., can you work out the name of the odd one out?

1, 12, 6, 15, 14, 26, 15

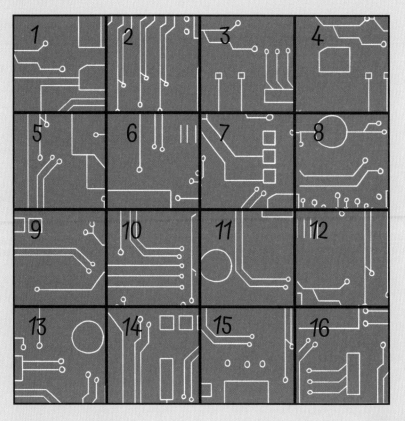

Circuit malfunction

This circuit board isn't working. It needs putting together in the correct order. Write the board numbers in the empty grid to show where they should go.

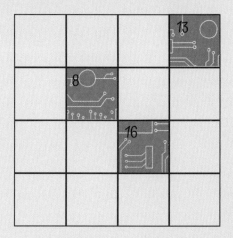

Special delivery

Help the delivery driver find the correct house number by reading the clues below.

14	15	20	21	22	25	26
34	35	39	41	45	49	55
71	73	84	87	88	89	91

1. The house number is an odd number.
2. It must be divisible by 7.
3. The second digit is more than double the first.

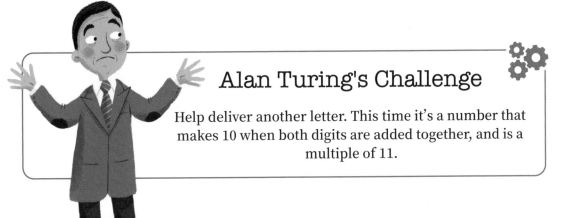

Alan Turing's Challenge

Help deliver another letter. This time it's a number that makes 10 when both digits are added together, and is a multiple of 11.

Twists and turns

This roller coaster is proving very popular! Who is already on the ride? Follow the lines to find out.

Seahorse match

Can you find the seahorse's true silhouette?

Alan Turing's Challenge

Pick one of the silhouettes and draw a seahorse
that would create this shape.

All in one

Can you draw the picture on the right without taking your pencil off the paper? It's trickier than it looks!

Alan Turing's Challenge

How many triangles can you see in this shape?

Hive sweet hive

Count the bees in the swarm to find
out which hive they belong to.

21

24

26

Changing room

Can you fit each item of furniture just once in each row and column? Sketch them in the empty squares.

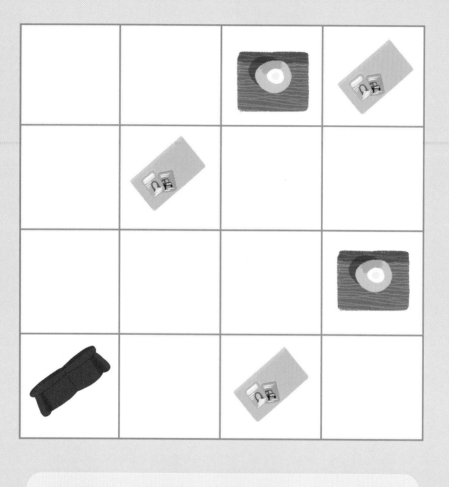

42

Lazy lions

What are the names of these characters? Imagine the hands of a clock and read the letters shown by the minute hand first. The first lion's name is shown by turning the hands to 7.05. The second lion's name is shown by 3.40. The zookeeper's name is shown by the time 11.15.

Alan Turing's Challenge

How many hours (on average) does a lion sleep for in a day? The number is above 15 but below 20. It cannot be divided by 8 and it is not a prime number.

Puzzle 1
$C \times E =$

Puzzle 2
$D + E =$

Puzzle 3
Puzzle 1 – Puzzle 2

Puzzle 4
$A + F =$

Puzzle 5
$H – E =$

Puzzle 6
Puzzle 4 – Puzzle 5

Puzzle 7
Puzzle 3 – Puzzle 6

8

12

1

5

2

Locked out

Lady Hamilton-Smythe's trinket box is locked with a padlock. Which one is it? The padlock matches the answer to Puzzle 7 on the left. Using the code a = 1, b = 2, c = 3, etc., replace each letter with a number to complete the calculations and work out which it is.

Equation motivation

Use the clues to help the scientist to circle the correct number. She has already had four guesses.

397   345   244   900   834
      723   194   553   627
            199

GUESS	CLUES
429	Two numbers correct, but not in the right position.
928	One number correct, but not in the right position.
128	One number correct, in the right position.
284	One number correct, in the right position.

Alan Turing's Challenge

One of the numbers in the yellow box is the answer to this calculation. Which number?

$$23 \times 5 \times 3$$

Book shuffle

Can you find all 10 differences between these two pictures?
Circle the differences in the picture on the right.

Escape plan

This explorer needs to find his way out of the cursed temple. Use the code and the phrase below to help him get from one orange hexagon to the other.

To find the path through the maze, replace each letter in the phrase at the bottom with a number. Use the code a = 1, b = 2, c = 3, etc.

Start

THIS PATH WILL LEAD YOU TO FREEDOM

Penguin pairs

Each of these penguins has a buddy that matches it perfectly. Match each one, then circle the odd one out.

Alan Turing's Challenge

If each penguin pair had a chick, how many penguins would there be altogether?

Movie mix-up

Help the friends get to the right movie screen. Write the numbers 1 to 4 in each row, column, and linked circles without a number repeating. The screen each friend needs is the number in their corner.

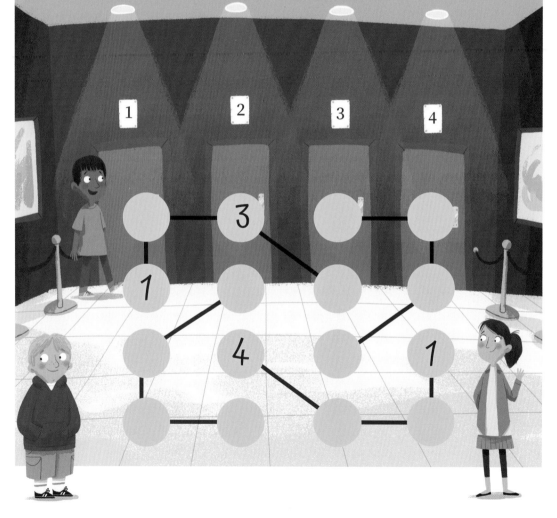

Cycle chase

Plot the path of this cycle race and discover where the cyclists finish. Use the compass to help you.

1 square = 1 mile

North 4 miles

East 3 miles

South 1 mile

West 2 miles

North 2 miles

East 3 miles

South 3 miles

West 3 miles

South 1 mile

Start

N
W ← → E
S

Alan Turing's Challenge

Ask a grown-up to help you find a compass (or use the compass app on a phone) to help you see where north, south, east, and west are in your own home. Can you plot the route from your kitchen to your bedroom? You might need to add directions for up and down as well.

Cupcake crazy

Make your way through the cake grid using the sequence of tasty cupcakes to the left. You can move up, down, and across, but not diagonally.

Start

Finish

Block chain

Use each of these shapes just twice to fill the grid. You can rotate and flip the shapes however you like.

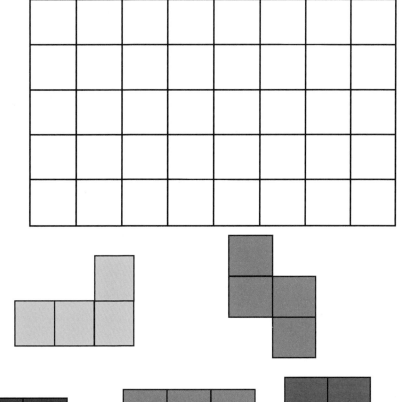

Alan Turing's Challenge

What is the tallest tower you can make with these five blocks? Draw it out on a blank sheet of paper. You can rotate any block but you cannot balance a block over an empty space.

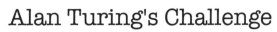

Screen break

Something has gone wrong with this phone!
Can you work out what the message should say?

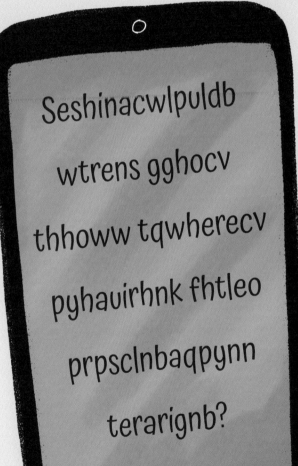

Seshinacwlpuldb

wtrens gghocv

thhoww tqwherecv

pyhavirhnk fhtleo

prpsclnbaqpynn

terarignb?

The message starts with an S. Cross out two letters, then write down the letter that follows it. Continue to the end of the message.

Going loco

All these words have something to do with trains.
Can you unscramble their letters?

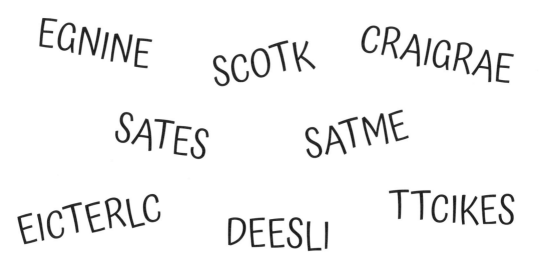

EGNINE

SCOTK

CRAIGRAE

SATES

SATME

EICTERLC

DEESLI

TTCIKES

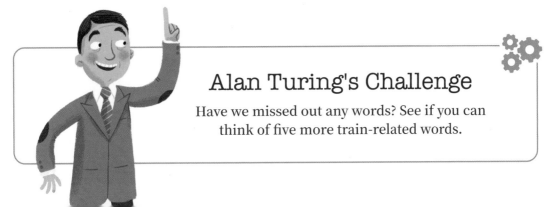

Alan Turing's Challenge

Have we missed out any words? See if you can
think of five more train-related words.

Mind fizzers

Think outside the box to answer these riddles.

1. What type of transport has eight wheels but can only carry one passenger?

2. Charlotte throws a ball as hard as she can. It comes back to her without bouncing off anything. How did she do it?

3. What has to be broken before it can be used?

4. Where does Friday come before Thursday?

5. What is as round as a saucepan and as deep as a sink but if you poured in all the oceans of the world, you could not fill it up?

Odd Squad

Megan can't find the rest of her team! Can you find six other players with the exact same uniform as her?

Megan

Alan Turing's Challenge

There are eleven players in a soccer squad. How many more players does Megan need?

Cut-up coconuts

This picture was taken at the fair, but it has been broken! Can you fit all the pieces back together? Which two pieces are not part of the picture?

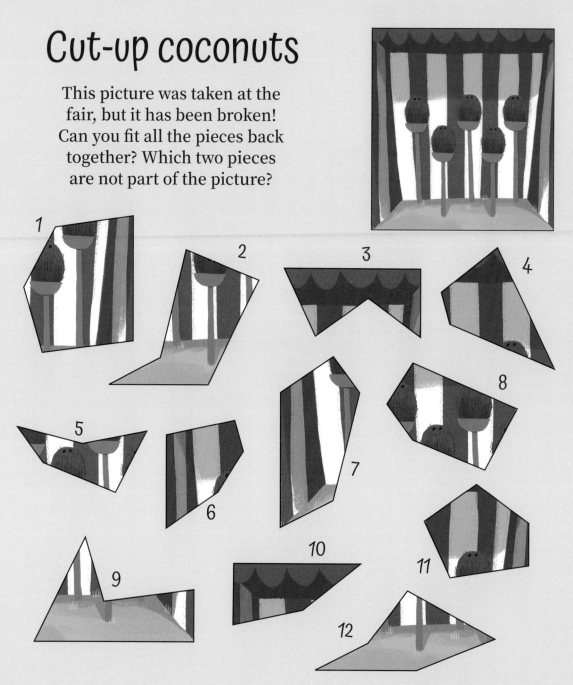

58

Haunted maze

Starting with the ghost in the bottom-left corner, follow the ghostly gazes to find your way through the maze to the finish.

Finish

Alan Turing's Challenge

Four of these ghosts will trap you in an infinite loop.
Can you find them?

Pet pixels

Fill in the squares on the right-hand side to make a reflection of the left-hand side and complete a pixel dog.

Stripy count up

Take a look at this zebra herd. How many can you count?

Alan Turing's Challenge

One of these zebras has a face that is slightly different from the rest. Can you spot it?

Frog hop

Fit each of these frogs once into every row and column. If you don't want to draw them, write pink, green, blue, or purple to show where they go.

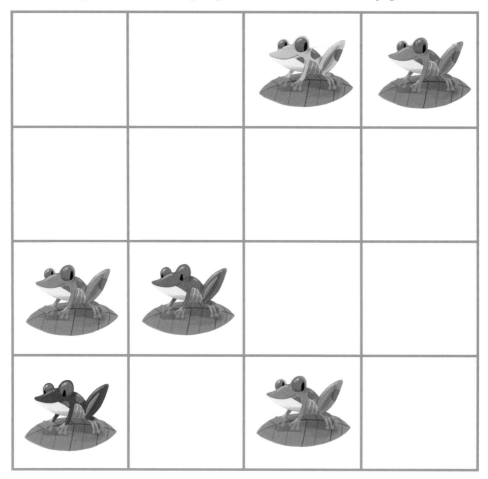

Shady forest

Can you match each
of these trees with its
identical silhouette?

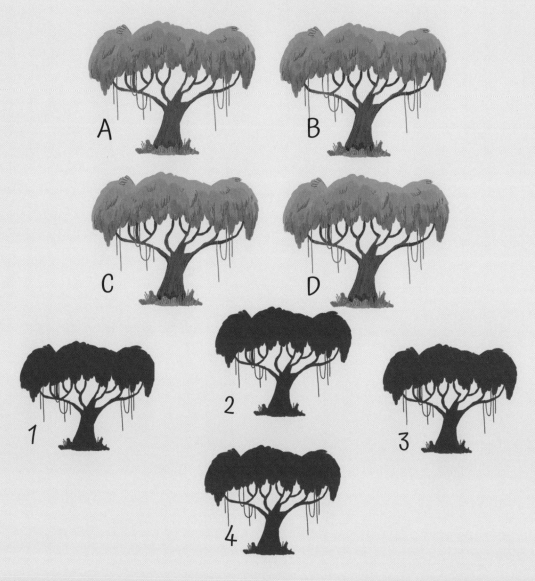

Diddy dino

This baby diplodocus is exploring.
Help him make his way through the maze.

Start

Finish

Fluttering butterflies

These butterflies might all look the
same, but one is slightly different.
Can you spot it?

Diner differences

Take a look at these busy diners. Can you find 8 differences in the second picture?

Busy day

This mermaid is busy visiting her friends. Use the clues to work out in what order she visits them.

She visits Bubbles before Sandy.

She visits Sandy before Coral.

She visits Pebbles after Sandy but before Coral.

The mermaid visits:

1.

2.

3.

4.

Starstruck

It's this fairy's job to balance the stars. Using three stars, how can she balance the last set of scales?

Tiny

Small

Medium

Large

Scale one:

Scale two:

Scale three:

Scale four:

Alan Turing's Challenge

Which stars could you use to balance eight tiny stars? There are four different ways you could do it.

Pick and mix

Can you find all of these patterns
of mini-treats in the large grid?

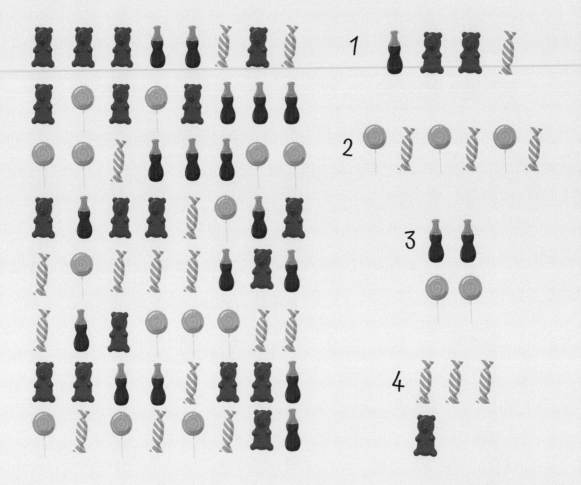

Mirror writing

These envelopes have been written back to front. Can you help the postal worker to figure out who they are addressed to?

TUTANKHAMUN
VALLEY OF THE
KINGS
EGYPT

DOCTOR FOSTER
GLOUCESTER
UK

UNCLE SAM
STARS AND STRIPES
STREET
USA

Alan Turing's Challenge

While you have your mirror out, check out this fun fact!

The first stamp produced was called the Penny Black!

See the sights

Mark all the coordinates on the grid, then join them in order to discover the route the tour bus will take. What shape does the route make?

Hint:
For coordinates, the first number is along the bottom.

3:1, 4:4, 1:7, 4:7, 6:10, 7:7, 10:7, 8:4, 9:1, 6:3, 3:1.

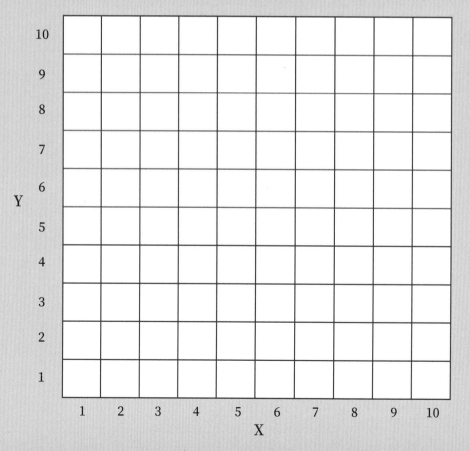

Lock down

Martin has forgotten his bike-lock code. It's one of the numbers below. Use the clues to work out which.

1135
8443
2486
2979
3931
4628
2864
4692
5413
4152

Clues:

The code contains an odd number.

All its numbers are different.

It contains a number higher than 5.

Alan Turing's Challenge

If the code was the highest number with all the digits added together which one would it be?

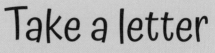

Take a letter

Mr. Patel has given each schoolkid their own letter on the register. Follow the lines to see which letter belongs to each child.

A

B

C

D

1

2

3

4

Broken pipes

Quick, fix the plumbing! Put the pipes back together before there's a flood!

Finish the grid by writing in the number of the squares in their correct positions.

Alan Turing's Challenge

How many valves can you see on the pipes? The valves look like small wheels—but you may only be able to see them from the side.

Wizardly wonder

Help the wizard put his magic numbers in order. Make sure each number is placed just once in each row, column, and linked circles.

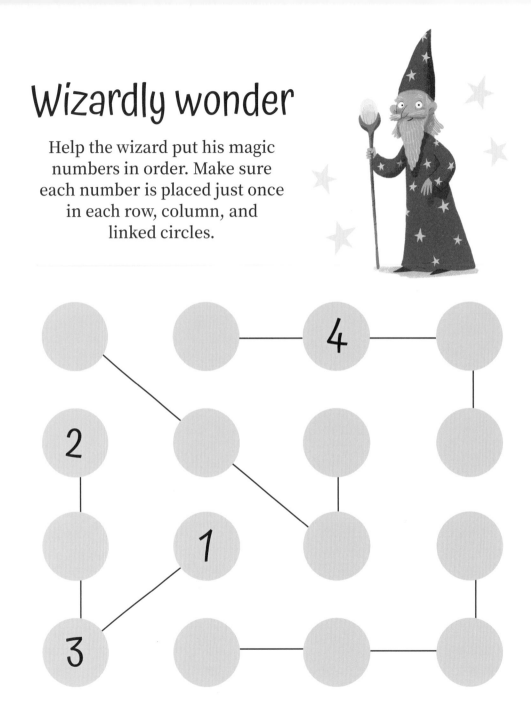

1

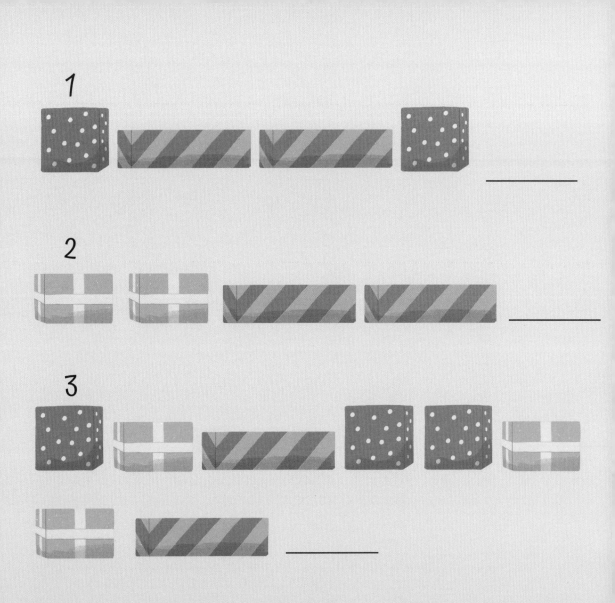

2

3

Present and correct

Which gift should come next in each sequence?

Look at these kite fliers!
Can you work out which
kite each of them owns,
and what their names are?

Kite strings

· Isabella is not wearing purple.

· Harper is waving.

· Ava's kite is not the bird.

· Isabella's kite is pink.

	Name			

Best laid plans

Take a look at this blueprint. Can you work out which house was built using this plan?

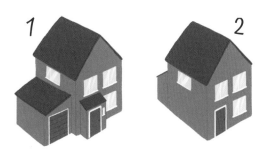

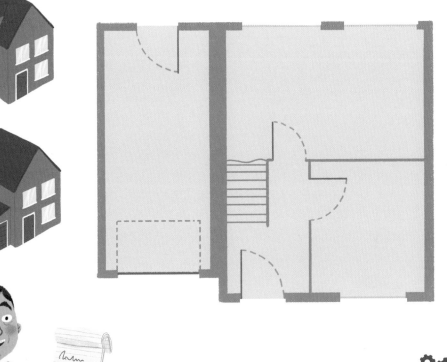

Alan Turing's Challenge

Pick one of the other houses and draw a blueprint for its design!

Dragon attack

Help the knight battle the dragons in the correct order. Use the clues below to help you.

She battled a dragon with blue wings first.

The smallest dragon was battled after the dragon breathing flames.

She battled the dragon with the arrow tail, last.

Alan Turing's Challenge

What percentage of the dragons have just two wings? What percentage of the dragons are breathing flames, and what percentage have a green body?

Number crunching

What is the largest number the scientist can make by moving one bar in this number?

Cut the cake

Can you put this delicious cake back in the correct order? Copy each number into the empty grid.

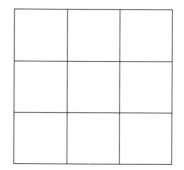

Alan Turing's Challenge

If this circular cake was cut into slices each with an angle of exactly 60°, how many slices would there be?

Greedy goats

These goats need feeding. Draw in a bag of oats for each goat. Each goat has at least one bag of oats in a square across or down from it. The oats do not touch each other's squares, not even diagonally. The numbers outside the grid show how many bags of oats are in each row or column. The first one has been done for you.

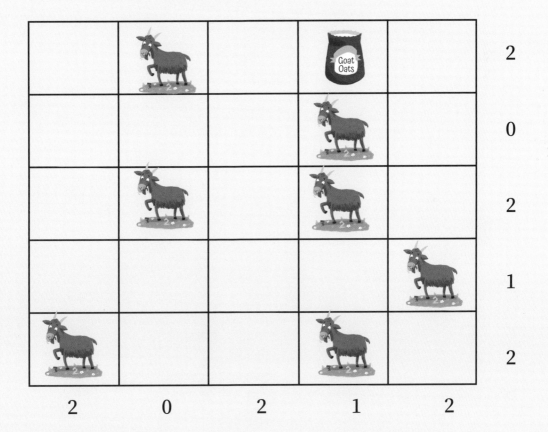

Peak Problem

This climbing picture has been spilt into 12 slices. What order should they be in from top to bottom?

1

2

3

4

5

6

7

8

9

10

11

12

Puzzle
SOLUTIONS!

No peeking here until you've given each puzzle your best shot! If you get stuck, try rereading the instructions carefully.

Solutions

Page 4

Alan Turing's Challenge
Two thousand, seven hundred.

Page 5

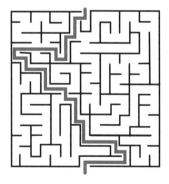

Page 6

Bolt	✕			
Megadroid			✕	
Robbo		✕		
Axel				✕

Page 7

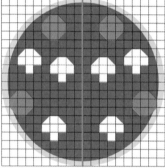

Alan Turing's Challenge
Pizza was the first item to be bought over the internet.

Page 8

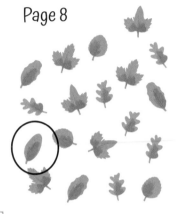

Page 9

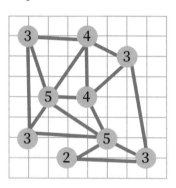

Alan Turing's Challenge
3

Solutions

Page 10

Page 11

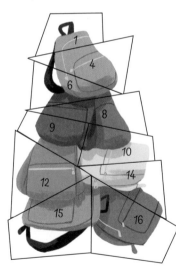

Alan Turing's Challenge

2, 3, 5, 7, 11, 13 are all prime numbers.

Page 12

1. Stairs
2. Towel
3. Jim
4. Are you asleep yet?
5. The dark
6. Second

Page 13

Monday:

Tuesday:

Wednesday:

Page 14

You have to cross out the second and third words for every three to read:

The tickets for today's concert have sold out. Try again tomorrow.

Page 15

Giraffe 3

Page 16

The mountaineers reached the summit at 1.15pm.

Page 17

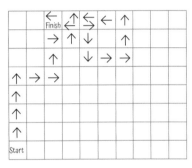

Page 19

Solutions

Page 20

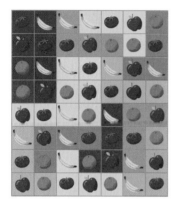

Page 21

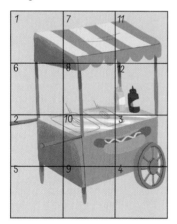

Alan Turing's Challenge
True.

Page 22

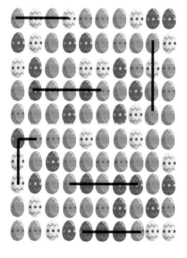

Page 23

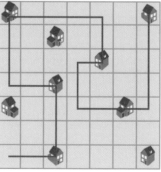

G7

Page 24

Fish 1 = 81 and should be blue

Fish 2 = 8 and should be green

Fish 3 = 17 and should be red

Fish 4 = 6 and should be green

Alan Turing's Challenge

Use the numbers in the order 8, 81, 6, and 17 to make the number 881,617

Page 25

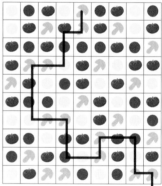

Solutions

Page 26

Page 27

= $6

= $10

= $8

Page 28

Here is one way. There are others.

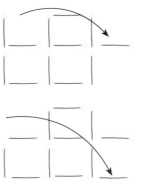

Alan Turing's Challenge

There are 4 small squares and 3 large squares.

Page 29

Number 4 fits perfectly.

Page 30

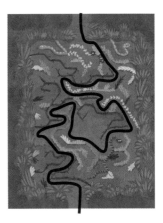

Page 31

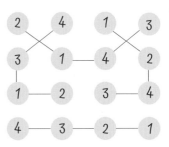

Solutions

Page 32

Bracelets: 9

Necklaces: 3

Rings: 9

Page 33

1. Your name
2. A clock
3. A cold
4. A coin
5. A secret
6. Short

Page 34

Page 35

8 has a shorter tongue.

Alan Turing's Challenge
Alfonzo

Page 36

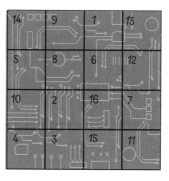

Page 37

49

Alan Turing's Challenge
55

Page 38

3

Page 39

Page 40

Here's one way. There are others.

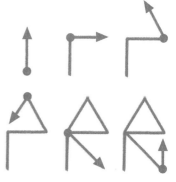

Alan Turing's Challenge

9: five small triangles, and four large triangles each made from two small triangles.'

Page 41

24

Solutions

Page 42

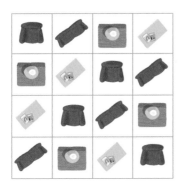

Page 44

Puzzle 1: C $\times$ E = 3 $\times$ 5 = 15.

Puzzle 2: D + E = 4 + 5 = 9.

Puzzle 3: Puzzle 1 – Puzzle 2 = 15 − 9 = 6.

Puzzle 4: A + F = 1 + 6 = 7.

Puzzle 5: H − E = 8 − 5 = 3.

Puzzle 6: Puzzle 4 – Puzzle 5 = 7 − 3 = 4.

Puzzle 7: Puzzle 3 – Puzzle 6 = 6 − 4 = 2.

Page 43

First lion: Loki

Second lion: Rori

Zookeeper: Davy

Alan Turing's Challenge

18 hours

Page 45

194

Alan Turing's Challenge

345

Page 47

Page 48

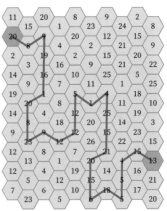

Solutions

Page 49

Alan Turing's Challenge
12

Page 50

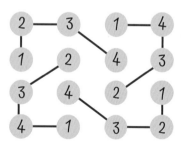

Page 51

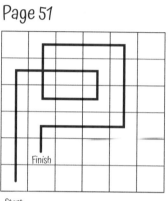

Finish

Start

Page 52

Page 53

Here is one solution. There are others.

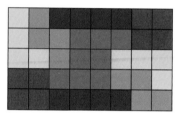

Alan Turing's Challenge

Here is one solution. There are others.

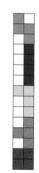

The tower is 15 blocks high.

Page 54

Shall we go to the park to play tag?

Solutions

Page 55

ENGINE, STOCK, CARRIAGE, SEATS, STEAM, ELECTRIC, DIESEL, TICKETS

Page 56

1. Roller skates.
2. She threw the ball straight up into the air.
3. An egg.
4. In a dictionary.
5. A sieve or a colander.

Page 57

Alan Turing's Challenge

4: Megan, the six players above, and another 4.

Page 58

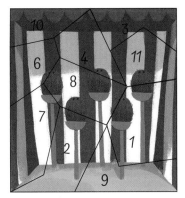

5 and 12 are not part of the picture.

Page 59

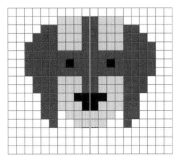

Page 60

Page 61

There are 32 zebras.

Alan Turing's Challenge

Solutions

Page 62

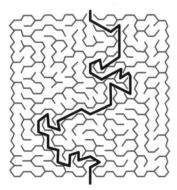

Page 63

A = 1
B = 4
C = 2
D = 3

Page 64

Page 65

Page 67

Page 68

1. Bubbles
2. Sandy
3. Pebbles
4. Coral

Page 69

Alan Turing's Challenge

1. One large star.
2. Two medium stars.
3. Two small stars and one medium star.
4. Eight tiny stars.

Page 70

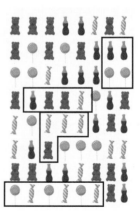

Solutions

Page 71

TUTANKHAMUN
VALLEY OF THE KINGS
EGYPT

DOCTOR FOSTER
GLOUCESTER
UK

UNCLE SAM
STARS AND STRIPES STREET
USA

Alan Turing's Challenge

The first stamp produced was
called the Penny Black!

Page 72

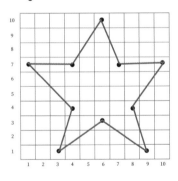

Page 73

4692

Alan Turing's Challenge

2979

Page 74

Page 75

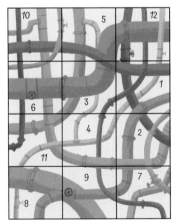

Alan Turing's Challenge

There are 7 valves.

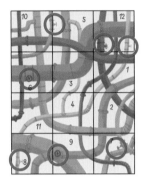

Page 76

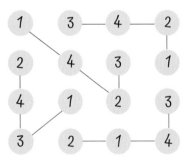

Page 77

1.

2.

3.

Solutions

Page 78

	Name	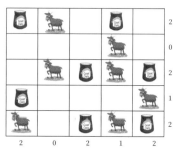		
	Isabella	✓		
	Harper			✓
	Ava		✓	

Page 79

House 4 matches the blueprint.

Page 80

The knight fought the dragons in the order C, A, D, B.

Alan Turing's Challenge

75% have just two wings.

25% are breathing flames.

50% have a green body.

Page 81

990

Page 82

Alan Turing's Challenge

There are 360° in a circle so there would be 6 × 60° slices.

Page 83

Page 84